55 Questions to Ask Yourself!

Across 8 Dimensions for A New You!

any policies, processes, or directions contained within is the solitary and utter responsibility of the recipient reader. Under no circumstances will any legal responsibility or blame be held against the publisher for any reparation, damages, or monetary loss due to the information herein, either directly or indirectly.

Respective authors own all copyrights not held by the publisher.

The information herein is offered for informational purposes solely, and is universal as so. The presentation of the information is without contract or any type of guarantee assurance.

The trademarks that are used are without any consent, and the publication of the trademark is without permission or backing by the trademark owner. All trademarks and brands within this book are for clarifying purposes only and are the owned by the owners themselves, not affiliated with this document.

TABLE OF CONTENTS

INTRODUCTION

I want to thank you and congratulate you for Purchasing the book, "55 Questions, Across 8 Dimensions for A New You!"

Do you know that questioning yourself is one of the powerful ways to unlock some hidden things about yourself that you never knew? By asking the right questions, you will unravel interesting versions of yourself. In this book, I have specially crafted coaching questions used by life coaches to unveil the answers from you.

I would recommend you to use a partner to question each other to get better results. It is all fine to go it alone, but you will make far more progress if you involve another person in the process. This is because we tend to answer in depth when someone else asks the question. We tend to think deeply so that the answers we provide are concise and complete. You may think that you are bringing clarity to the other person but the truth is you are bringing clarity to yourself.

Before we can dive into the meat of this book, here are a few coaching tips:

Make sure the other person is in a comfortable place and is ready to be completely involved in the conversation; make sure to put the phones in silent mode and to achieve the best results, make sure you write the answers in a piece of paper. Not only will the latter ensure your answers are written down in an organized, well-structured manner, but you will be able to keep the piece of paper around for future reference.

Thanks again for purchasing this book. I hope you enjoy it!

1. SELF-DISCOVERY

It is only fitting that we start by covering, and exhausting, self-image. After all, you could have perfect expression in every other area of your life but if your self-image is unsatisfactory to you, you will never be completely at peace with yourself and to properly reconcile with your abilities and uniqueness. Therefore, you need to first fix any self-image issues you may have and everything else becomes remarkably simple to tackle.

So how do you view yourself?

It is important to mention that how you view yourself matters more than how others view you. You need to be completely in touch with yourself to achieve anything great. Some people might attend seminars or workshops, read numerous books, have enough knowledge but still lack wisdom! The reason is that they didn't change the existing self-image which is not supporting them to achieve their goals. These people spend years and years running around, trying to gather knowledge from every source they can access, but they never succeed in plugging the hole in their soul.

What these people do not understand is that trying to change the outside world rather than focusing on themselves, is like trying to change the image in the mirror rather than themselves. It is an exercise in folly, and really the only way to get results from this kind of thing is to blatantly lie to yourself... which we all know is not possible. Eventually, you will walk back to the mirror and see the same image you convinced yourself to have changed staring back at you. If you want a solution, you have to follow a more permanent route.

Do you want to know how you view yourself? Do you want to know who you are, at least as for now? Look at the areas of your life, such as your relationships, your career Etc. Get a proper feel of who you are by asking questions and answering them honestly in these areas of your life. Afterward, you will have the arsenal you need to make the requisite changes, and become a better you.

Here are questions you need to ask yourself, in your examination of your self-image-

1. Who am I?

This one, really, is the mother of all self-image questions. *Who are you? What is it that defines you? If you were to die today, and the gravestone engraver was given all the material he needed to describe you on your gravestone, what would he write? What would you write about yourself if you were the engraver of your own gravestone?*

There are no hard and fast rules when it comes to answering this one. You can choose to dig up your history back to 7 generations of your family and begin constructing an answer from that point if you want. Alex Haley had to dig deep into his history to truly define himself. While it was quite difficult at some point, the answers he was able to derive were so rich in substance that they enriched him and then spilled over to enrich the rest of the world.

Define who you are in your own way. Seek to describe yourself as clearly as you can. Feel free to use your environment in your bid to define who you are. Once you are able to answer this question, answering every other question about you becomes significantly easier, and you are able to carry yourself with full confidence when doing so.

2. How do I view myself? Positive or negative?

This is yet another question that requires you to have a hard look into your life. You probably already have a general view of whether your life is positive or negative, but look deeply into your life nonetheless, and see if you can revise your opinion.

Is your life unrolling negatively or positively? Have you made sufficient progress to call yourself a success, or at least a relative success, in your own terms? A great point to start at is to ask yourself if you have met the goals you had in mind 5 years, 3 years ago, 2 years ago and finally a year ago, for your present life stage. *Are you satisfied with your current station in life, going by those goals?*

Please remember that your goals do not have to be only career-oriented- you could have had weight loss goals, sports-related goals, family/relationship related goals, travel-related goals, Etc. Also ask yourself if you are pleased with how you relate with other people around you, and most importantly if you express yourself to them in a way that leaves you feeling satisfied.

Sometimes, in order to answer this question satisfactorily, you have to examine things/points/factors/people in your life that you are happy or unhappy and resentful about. Many times, you will discover that the happiness or unhappiness is really directed at yourself, and the external elements are just that, external elements. Depending on the scale of your emotions you will be able to answer this question with more conviction.

3. Who are your top 3 role models?

This one is usually quite fun, especially if you have a knack for examining others' lives and drawing inspiration from them.

Who are your top 3 role models? Who are those people who have conducted their lives in a way that you believe would be ideal for you? These people could be successful career people. They could also be people who stay fit 360 days a year or people who have managed to carve out a lifestyle that you desire, however simple and un-fancy it may be.

Start by drawing up a list of 10, if you have a lot to choose from, and gradually cut down this number to three.

4. What are those qualities that you admire in them?

Examine the qualities of your role models and determine what qualities draw you so powerfully to them. They could be people who project great warmth and calm even in the face of hostility, like Gandhi. They could have shown great patience and resistance to pain and suffering, like Mandela. They could display great work ethic and stamina that you have come to appreciate. Focus on the qualities that intrigue you about them the most and then list them down.

Remember that your greatest role models could be members of your family who provide a close example of what you desire to accomplish. Therefore, even as you look far and wide for solid role models, look close too, for the greatest answers sometimes lie close to home.

5. What are your top 3 strengths?

Focus on your life, and determine what you are best at. You may need to take some time to answer this one, especially if you are a multi-talented individual, but this one should be relatively easy to answer.

You could be a really social person who is very good at striking up a conversation and lighting up a room. You could be very adept at speaking or you could be great at analysis and research, Etc. These qualities do not have to be qualities that everybody recognizes in you. Sometimes; your best-kept secret could be your greatest asset. At the end of the day, there is no one person who knows you quite as well as yourself.

6. What are the top obstacles that you have overcome? How did you do so?

You surely have obstacles that you have had to overcome, at some time or other. *What are they and just how did you manage to overcome them?* Feel free to reflect as far back in your life as you want. It could be that you had some really hard conundrums to circumvent when you were a child, at least on a childhood scale, and acknowledge that you held up nicely.

Walt Disney, of Disney fame, loved to say that he wrestled so much with challenges as a child that his adult life was relatively easy in comparison. He said that his days as a kid, doing the newspaper route with extra newspaper wrapped beneath his jacket to keep out the fierce winter cold, far outmatched his adult years in terms of hardship.

Perhaps, you have such a backstory. List down your biggest obstacles faced, and how you overcame them. Take as much time as you need to reflect.

7. What do you love doing? (In terms of career and passion)

Your career, as you may already know by now, does not define you. You are so much more than your present career, even though you may be active in a field that you really like. But it helps to define what line you really want to operate in, as far as your career and passion go.

What is it that you love doing? It does not have to be an occupation that the whole of society lauds. You do not have to make such choices as 'lawyer', 'doctor', Etc. If you like to draw/paint, then be proud to mention this. If you love sports and intend to carve a career out of a sport, be confident and apply yourself similarly.

If you love working with cars, then this is what you should list. Remember that you cannot really lie to yourself; so list down what you really love doing, and not what your family and peers would love you to do.

8. What do you like about yourself?

There may be a lot of things that you like about yourself... list all of them down. *Do you like how you look? Are you impressed with your height? Does your style of dress fill you with confidence? Do you like that you think fast on your feet? Do you like your abstract, creative nature?* Perhaps, you like how you relate with your entire family and the way you have built and nurtured relationships with them over the years.

List down every quality you love about yourself, and do not feel vain while at it; there is no vanity in recognizing things that you love about yourself. After all, it is most likely the case that you have had to work hard to develop these things.

9. What makes you lose track of time?

No, we are not talking about what distracts you and takes your mind off of meaningful work. I am talking about a fierce hobby/ passion/ recreational activity that fulfills you to such a degree that whenever you indulge in it, you are in your own little world for a while. For some people, it is video games, while others derive that sort of intense preoccupation with more technical activities like coding, painting and golfing.

10. If money was abundant in your life what would you do?

This question will help you discover who you are far better than most others will. Because by answering this question, you unearth your greatest desires. At the same time, you are able to see what your personality traits would be if allowed to manifest without being impeded. *Would you splash the money on vehicles and homes? Would you save up most of it and guarantee security into old age? Would you channel a good amount of it toward charity? Would you seek to get back at those who have hurt you in the past?* Seek to answer this question as concisely as possible.

11. What is that one thing that you continue doing even if you have all the riches in the world?

There has to be something that you are doing today that you would continue doing if you managed to amass all the wealth in the world. *What is this thing? Does it involve your career? Is it family oriented? Is it a hobby?* A good point to start at is to ask yourself what things fulfill you the most. You can then refine your way to one definitive answer.

12. What completes you as a person?

For some people, family is what completes them. Some people are incomplete without their jobs and the exhilarating challenges that come with them. There are some people who do not feel complete without their wardrobes. There is no shameful answer. Ask yourself what completes you, and allows you to be at your best behavior at all times. Ask yourself what element in your life leaves the biggest void when it isn't there.

13. What are you complimented for usually?

There will be that one thing that people compliment you for. You could be really good at speaking, art, making and reciting poetry, relating to people, sports Etc. Your answer should be unique to you. Think of that one thing that you get numerous compliments for- that one thing that draws attention to you, and then list it down.

Let us now move on to goals and what questions you need to ask yourself about your goals:

2. GOAL QUESTIONS

"Clarity is power" - Tony Robbins

It is important to have clear goals and objectives. You need to be clear about your goals, to truly arrive at your destination. You cannot afford to have unclear goals. Not only will you not be able to properly focus and put in the requisite work, but people who are not clear on what they want rarely achieve what they desire because they do not know even what that is.

It is really important to know where you are heading towards. It's like you have an amazing private jet fitted with all those little tweaks that make it exceptional but ultimately have no clear plan for its use. You are never sure where to go with it.

Ultimately, as enviable and phenomenal this jet may be, it will only end up being a money drain. Have in mind that this very machine would be wondrous and extremely fast and efficient if you had clear destinations for it. Think of your body and brain as the private jet, and your life goals as the destinations.

Here are questions that will help bring about clarity to your goals and objectives:

14. What fulfills me as an individual?

What career fulfills you as a person? What is your passion? There is that special choice of career that you have been passionate about for as long as you can remember. When you are working at it, it is as if you are not working but rather having intense, goal-oriented fun. This one should be clear and easy to mark out unless you are a typical multi-talented individual. If this describes you, you may need to sit for a while and strain out your options through a mental sieve so that you have one clear, outstanding one, or make room for two or more choices.

Of course, it helps to have the main choice, and maybe have a 2nd or 3rd choice, but with the bulk of your attention going to your main choice.

15. What skills do I have to achieve this goal?

If you are passionate about something, then you may have worked on a few of its facets already, seeing as you have a genuine passion for it. In addition, you may already naturally possess qualities that equip you wonderfully for your career choice/goal. For example, you may be good at business transactions and salesmanship; traits which will undoubtedly help you if your goal is to be a super successful businessperson.

You may possess very well-coordinated hands that will serve you well if your goal is to be an artist. It could be that you have great stamina, which will aid you in truly making your mark as an athlete. Examine the qualities and skills you bring to the table and see which ones support your goal.

16. Why else would I need to achieve this goal?

This is also known as seeking a 2nd supporting reason for accomplishing a goal, which will back up and boost your original reason/set of reasons. For example, it could be that you want to achieve your goal so that you can afford a mortgage, pay off school debts, etc. However, it could be that your parents or siblings are ailing, or could use your help. Seek out a

2nd supportive reason- even a 3rd- and list it down. It could provide an extra dimension to your goals, as well as extra motivation to achieve them.

17. When do I want to achieve this?

They say that a goal cannot really qualify as one if it is not defined by a timeframe. It is vital that you know exactly when you want to accomplish your goal. *When do you want to hit your goals? How many weeks/months/years should it take?* Make sure that you define your goal with a proper timeframe. The specificity will add even more fuel to your fire, and fill you with the conviction that indeed, you can truly live your dreams.

18. What would happen if I achieve this goal?

There are multiple scenarios that could unravel once you do achieve your goal. Of course, the most obvious one is a sense of fulfillment and accomplishment. Accomplishing your goal could mean that you never had to work a regular day job again, or that you were finally able to clear off debt that you had for years.

Accomplishing your goal could make the difference in how you view yourself; it could transform you from a loser to a winner in your eyes. List every possible thing that is likely to happen once you achieve your goal; list as many as you can. This will help you construct a clear, concise picture of the future, and what it could hold in store for you.

19. How would your surroundings change when you achieve this goal?

By surroundings, I mean environment, and by environment, I do not just mean the physical features that surround you, I also mean the people around you, the circumstances that have governed you all this time, family, workmates Etc.

What happens when you achieve your goals? What changes? How does your success influence your environment? It could be that achieving your goal compels you to change location, or jobs, to accommodate the developments in your life.

While the external elements really do not mean as much as the internal ones, it helps to consider them so that you can be better prepared for the future.

20. What would you see, hear and feel once you achieve this goal?

This is related to the previous question- *what feedbacks will your surroundings give to you and your senses?* You may also consider what you will personally feel, hear and see and base all of it exclusively on your perspective. Evaluate these things- when the time comes and you meet your goal, you will be pleasantly surprised when you feel the exact same experiences you listed down.

21. How would you remind yourself to stay on track during the journey?

Here is something you should know; you will come across multiple distractions on your path to your goal. You will require reminding yourself constantly to buckle down and get back to work. You will need to be vigilant at this, especially since the human brain is wired to seek short-term rewards first and long-term goals secondarily. Figure out a reminder plan; formulate a set of reminders that will keep you plugged in so that you do not get derailed.

With that out of the way, the next thing you need to determine is your beliefs and values.

3. Belief and Value Questions

"The only limits you have are the limits you believe" - Wayne Dyer

Each one of us is different; each one of us is unique. We all have traits that define us and separate us from everybody else. We have our own good and bad traits. We also possess certain beliefs and values which we are not aware of. Some beliefs might be helpful while some might be destructive. Still, these beliefs define you- they make up your core and determine what your psyche is like. This is why it is important to go about life without tripping over yourself apologizing at every turn.

This book is not trying to convince you to be a jerk; rather, you need to look at yourself as a unique being with a unique set of beliefs, traits, and desires. They do not make you a good or bad person- they only make you a person.

Anybody who tries to place hard and fast rules about how you should be and live your life is really just being quite frankly, ridiculous. You should aim to live life on your terms; aim to live life without any limits.

If people want to limit their lives by clinging onto beliefs that are self-defeating, they should do so by all means but they shouldn't try to impose their limits onto you, and you shouldn't let them anyway. After all, not only is life short, you only have one life to live. Reconcile yourself to the fact that you will indeed die one day; therefore, *why not live as full a life as possible?*

Let us look at some questions, which if you answer truthfully, you will understand your beliefs and values.

Questions you need to ask yourself

22. What do you stand for?

What is it that you stand for? Basically, what do you believe in? There are so many potential answers to this question. You can examine your religious beliefs and give an answer based on it. You can look to such societal and economical constructs as socialism and capitalism and determine where your allegiances lie. You can look to such ideals as privacy, or a lack of it and see where you fit, etc.

Basically, you have a code that you live by, made up of beliefs that you abide by. You are unique in that while you may possess similarities with other people, it is almost impossible to come across somebody who possesses a completely similar set of beliefs to yours.

Determine what you believe in and write it down. Ensure that you explore as many categories as you want to so that you can have a picture that is as clear and defined as possible.

23. What irritates you the most?

There are things that definitely rub you the wrong way, and surely there are a few that you can list out loud without having to do too much thinking. *Do you abhor your private business being made public for all and sundry to bear witness? Do you hate noisy people?* Perhaps, the unlikely things are the ones that irritate you the most, such as extreme concern from well-meaning people. It could be that you absolutely hate the sound of slamming doors, and you have known times when you were unable to focus for hours because somebody slammed one too hard.

Draw up a list of the things that irritate you the most, and then whittle down everything until you have a list of the top 5 most irritating things/elements/behaviors.

24. What are you ready to fight for?

They say that a person who is ready to fight for a few things that he/she finds ideal is a person who has found a set of things that will fulfill their soul. Surely, you have something/some things that you are willing to fight for. You have some beliefs that you are willing to stand up for in case you feel they are being belittled or unfairly criticized. Make up a small, yet concise list of these beliefs or ideals.

25. What does a successful person mean to you?

It will help you to answer this question from multiple angles. *What does a successful person look like to you, physically? How does he or she carry him/herself? How do they dress? Move on to the character traits; how do they generally respond to their environment? How do they respond to people, situations and their immediate environment? When faced with problems, what is their standard reaction? How much net worth does a successful person have, by your metric? What is the successful person's influence over his/her family, and how does he/she manage their familial affairs*?

Seek to answer this question by looking at every facet you can come up with so that the mental image you conjure is as clear and powerful as possible.

26. What is the difference between the present you and the successful you?

Answering the previous question should help you tremendously here. You already have a clear image of what a successful person looks like. *It is now time to see how you compare to that image. If the successful person has a trim physique, how does your own body compare? How does your wardrobe compare? How does your relationship with your family members compare? How does your bank account compare?*

Examine every facet that you explored in your quest to determine what a successful person is to you, and compare your equivalent honestly. This way, you will know where you truly stand, and what you need to do to improve.

27. What is holding me back to take actions?

What factors are holding you back? Is your physical environment holding you back? Is your partner partly responsible for your stagnation? Perhaps members of your family are blocking your progress?

Seek to have definitive answers to this one. For most of us, it is the fear of the unknown that blocks us; fear of embarrassment, ridicule, and failure as well. As somebody once said, once you know; then you know, and nobody can take that away from you.

28. What do you need to change mentally?

This question is linked to the previous one. Once you determine the mental aspects that are blocking you from succeeding, then it becomes easy to mark out the mental elements that you need to work on.

Ultimately, you know yourself best; therefore, determine what needs to be changed mentally so that you can actually target it and make the necessary changes.

29. How would you do them?

The next step is to determine how you would go about making these mental changes. Let us go back to our anxiety example; you could opt for a mix of meditation, and exercise. You could even opt to binge on motivational speeches and videos. If you have deep-seated anger issues that have gotten in the way of progress, you could opt for therapy sessions with a psychologist, or even just discuss the underlying experiences that brought your anger about with a close, trusted friend.

This is a very important step; you could know exactly what the problem is, but you are only halfway home if you cannot figure out how to confront and destroy the problem.

30. What habits do you need to change?

The best definition of what a habit is that- *a habit is a set of behaviors that are directly inspired by your beliefs. These beliefs ultimately translate to actions which are governed by the behaviors that these underlying beliefs compel*.

Basically, your habits, rather than have their core exist externally, on such elements as monetary or relationship success, they have an internal core and are constructed around your beliefs.

You are already familiar with your good and bad habits but if you are unsure about any one of them, look at your set of beliefs and look to see what habits they might inspire. Nevertheless, pinpoint the negative habits, such as procrastination, and look to eliminate them from your day to day life.

31. How would you change the habits you need to change?

Breaking a bad habit can be extraordinarily tough. But in truth, habit-breaking is often problematic because so many people go about it the wrong way. Rather than merely focus on what habits and routines to stop following, have a ready substitute for each habit you are looking to eliminate.

For example, if you want to break your habit of sleeping late, rather than simply say you want to sleep early, why not have a habit such as *"I will be in bed by 9.30 pm, and I will leave the laptop and Smartphone on my desk?"*

Also, it is vital that you understand what the habit you are looking to break 'means'. For instance, *what does laziness mean to you?* Your definition of being lazy could be working 8-hour days, instead of your preferred 14 hours. Be specific.

32. What is your favorite animal? And why?

This looks like an out of place question but it has its uses. If your favorite animal is the lynx, then thinking of it will help you envision its sleek, assertive nature, and then superimpose the image in your head onto your own life.

Some successful people have admitted to drawing up vivid imagery of their favorite animal, or spirit animal, before tackling challenging jobs or addressing huge crowds. This could work for you as well.

33. If you should describe yourself in a single word, what would that be?

The idea is to confine the description to one word. You could be assertive, calm, quiet, brooding, aggressive, tough, introverted... the list is endless. Examine your life thoroughly and determine what word describes you best. It may also help to determine the word you would like to describe yourself in the future so that you know what to work toward.

Unstuck Questions

There may be some past memories which hold you back from achieving your goal. Due to society, we tend to take information which is blocking us from achieving our goals too seriously, and too much to heart. This ends up hurting us and our progress.

These questions will help you unplug from this hamster wheel. Answer them as simply as you can, and feel free to derive answers from the previous questions in this chapter

What is stopping me?

Where do my thoughts ponder most of the time?

"I should always _____"

"I should never _____"

It is best that you come up with terse, pithy one-line answers for these unstuck. This will greatly simplify your vision, and you will have a clearly defined target to aim for.

The next section will focus on opportunities questions that you need to answer so that you can take advantage of opportunities around.

And hey, If you are enjoying reading this book, do leave you honest review on amazon.

4. OPPORTUNITY QUESTIONS

No matter your current stage in life, you have opportunities. What most of us fail to understand, is that we are flooded with opportunities. No matter where you are in life; no matter how bleak everything seems, if you have the means to access this book, no matter how undemanding they are, then you have more than enough opportunities around you to capitalize on and make a difference.

It helps to perform a thorough internal investigation, so that you can fully understand yourself, and where you are. When you are familiar with this, then you will most certainly know where you are coming from. When you know where you are coming from, it is a lot easier to determine exactly where you are going, and how you can capitalize on any opportunities in your way. This is why it is so important to ask yourself the questions in this book- they help you understand yourself better, which allows you to understand the environment, and the opportunities within it, better.

Eliminating excuses to be able to seize opportunities

Excuses are your enemy, no matter how much better they make your temporary situation. Especially if you live in a 1st world country like the US, it boggles the mind as to how you can excuse yourself for not meeting your goals and dreams.

You may not have much money, but it is generally easy to take care of your basic needs. In fact, the biggest challenge most people face is being able to properly manage their time.

If you look deep into any excuses you insist on clinging onto, you will quickly find that most of them are flimsy. The first step is admitting that you have perhaps not been good enough; that you have perhaps been wasteful and a bit of a slacker. Once this is out of the way, you will have a clean canvas on which to paint a new life picture.

Let's answer these questions to get insights into the opportunities that we have currently-

34. What could you do to change this situation?

Take a look at your current situation in life. *What is it that you could do to change it? If you are broke, what are some of the short term and long-term fixes that you could implement to make your financials look up? Perhaps you can pick up a 2nd job? Maybe you should commit to logging in extra hours at work, and taking advantage of the extra time? Could you perhaps get an extra degree to help you climb up the ladder faster in the future?*

Really, you can come up with as many potential solutions to your current situation. All you need to do is ponder broadly and exercise patience when writing down your solutions. Eventually, the ideas will come. List down as many of them as possible, and then pare them down so that you are only left with the most applicable solutions to work with.

35. What resources do you have currently to achieve your goals?

What elements do you have in your life that will help you get to your goals? You may need to think outside the box to mark them out. Your environment could be your biggest resource- it could be quiet, serene and full of like-minded people with similar goals to yours. It could be that your family is a great resource, pitching in when necessary to help you achieve your goals. Perhaps, you have connections with people in your line of work that will help you get to your destination. Your local library could be a phenomenal resource, with its stacks of books and research papers. Everything can be a resource; it just has to be effective enough in helping you move forward.

36. What else could you do to reach this goal?

There are a couple of ways to go about answering this question. First, you could ask yourself how you could stack up available resources to help you get to your goal. For instance, if your environment is not something you can call a resource with any conviction, you can move to a new neighborhood or town that offers more opportunities. If your friends are the opposite of resourceful, you could consider your relationships and make more useful friends. You could work an extra job to get more money, so you can take the necessary risks to achieve your goals. The other way you can answer this question is by looking inward and asking yourself what needs to change. If you are only working 6 hours a day, perhaps bumping this up to 10 hours will help you do more. If you go to bed with your tablet and computer, so that you almost always end up sleeping late and waking up late, you could consider leaving them in your desk and being in bed by 9.00 pm.

37. Whom can you get help from?

They say that no man is an island. Think of people who can help you get forward. Your family members could be excellent for this. Perhaps, you have friends who could be useful. Maybe you know someone with experience in your field that you could be a protégé to. Think hard, and then approach the names you come up with, with assertiveness and confidence. You will quickly realize that most people are eager to help and impart advice since they benefit from it as well.

38. Which options do you think would be the effective one?

As I said, you ought to draw up as many options for each question posed as possible. But it is hard to apply all of them, and at some point, redundancy begins to set in any way. Go through all the questions posed in this chapter with a fine toothcomb and begin by trimming down everything to a list of 5 top/most effective ones.

39. What do you think is required to speed up this process?

Often times, this primarily points to the sacrifices that you have to make. Really, making sacrifices is the greatest way to move forward. Nikola Tesla, perhaps the most intelligent man to live and Earth's greatest innovator, made a huge sacrifice in giving up his patent rights so that his AC concept of electricity could go through faster, and a power plant could be set up. Look at the areas you can make sacrifices in; sometimes it is as easy as sleeping fewer hours, and list them down.

If you don't take action, you will not change and you life will remain the same. The following chapter will focus on asking questions with regard to taking action and answering these questions will enable you to take the requisite action to achieve your goals.

5. ACTION QUESTIONS

"Ideas are shit, Execution matters"

- Gary Vee

Of course, ideas aren't really 'shit'. What Gary Vee means is that you could come up with all the ideas in the world, and they could be some of the greatest ideas that were ever drawn up, but without executing them, they are mostly useless. Ideas only get you through halfway; you need to execute them to really succeed.

Have you witnessed a person who appears to be perfectly set up for life, even with a lack of money; they are brilliant thinkers, eloquent in nature, well put together and capable of coming up with great ideas and analysis, but they can never seem to rise above their stage in life and exploit their advantages?

If you look deeply, you might discover that their greatest problem is that they can never seem to execute their brilliant ideas. Perhaps, they lack the requisite confidence and aggression to actually apply their ideas and see some fruits. Perhaps, their fear of failure is so crippling that they would rather eliminate all risk of failure by doing nothing than take a chance at success by executing their ideas.

It is not the one who holds new ideas that wins, but the one who executes them. Many people fall into the pit of over-thinking and analyzing but never take the most important step that is action. It is necessary to have clarity for sure, but knowledge would pay its price once you begin to take actions.

Here are some questions that you need to ask yourself, that will help you make the necessary steps to transition to action:

40. What do I want to achieve in 6 months?

Some people will tell you to start with a 10-year plan and then work your way down. But so many things could change within 10 years. You will grow older, and your view on life could change drastically somewhere in the middle. The best point to start at is the 6-month point. Look at it this way; 6 months is actually quite a long time. 6 months is around 24 weeks; 24 weeks is 180 days. If you focus properly for 180 days, then you could get a lot done in 180 days. Ask yourself what you want to have achieved in that span of time and write it down in bold.

41. What do I want to achieve in 3 months?

The next step to take is to split the 6-month block in half. *What is it that you want to achieve in 3 months? 3 months will mean 90 days- what would you like to have achieved in 90 days?* Of course, your 3-month goal should be relative to your 6-month goal.

However, as you may already know by now, drawing up your 3-month goal will not necessarily mean halving your 6-month goal. It is not always quite as simple as that, as some goals tend to progress in compound form.

Examine your 6-month goal thoroughly and then figure out how much work needs to be done within the 3-month period. It could even be that you ought to have completed all the work in 3 months, and focus on refining, editing, and marketing in the 3 months that follow. You know the nature of your goal best; break it down and come up with a viable 3-month goal.

42. What do I want to achieve in 1 month?

The next step is to decide where you want to be in 1 month. *How much of your 6-month goal should you have down in 1 month?* Again, like we said, it really isn't as simple as performing simple multiplication and division to come up with your mini goal. Examine your 3-month goal and then figure out how much each month ought to contribute to it. Focus on this month; focus on the resources at your disposal, time available, helpful models in place, etc. Take every element you can draw up into consideration, and then look to see if you can come up with a viable 1-month plan.

43. What do I want to achieve this week?

Next up, you need to figure out what you need to accomplish this week. And by the way, please be realistic. Given that you are just starting out, you may need to focus more on shaking off the cobwebs and getting up to speed with your scheduling.

If you are used to working for 6 hours, and you have decided to bump this up to 10 hours, best believe that you will not adapt seamlessly. You will struggle in the first couple of weeks, but everything will become easier.

It is advisable that you begin by setting a low target for your first week and keep scaling up over time. Use your first week to 'feel out' your new schedule, mindset, etc. Use it as training week. In fact, you can use the 1st month as training time. This way, you will avoid having to make abrupt stops every few weeks as you struggle to figure something new out and adjust to it.

44. What are the resources that I need to stay on track?

We covered the resources at your disposal in the previous chapter. You now have to figure out the resources that you NEED in order to stay as distraction-free as possible. Perhaps, you absolutely need to change your location. Perhaps, you need to set up an exclusive working space at home and install soundproofing. Maybe you require a small loan to help you make the next step. Examine your goal and then figure out the resources that you need. Write them down and then figure out how to access them

45. What would keep me from taking actions? And how do I deal with it?

Distractions will always come up. By the way, this will happen as sure as the sun rises and sets; you will get distracted multiple times, and each distraction will potentially deliver a hit to the prospect of accomplishing your goal. It will help to prepare beforehand for these distractions. List every potential distraction you can think of, and then formulate plans on how to curb each one of them. This way, when these distractions roll around, you will be prepared to handle them quickly and efficiently.

Get the best result by thinking on paper. If you are loving this book than am sure that you will love "Know Thyself journal" available at amazon. It is an updated version of this book with 99 questions and space for you to self-reflect. It is available now at Amazon.

6. HABIT QUESTIONS

"Success is really nothing more than the progressive realization of a worthy ideal. This means that any person who knows what they are doing and where they are going is a success." - Earl Nightingale

Look at Earl Nightingale's quote above- he does not say that success is **the utter realization** of a worthy ideal, but he says it is the *progressive realization* of a worthy ideal.

Basically, unlike what most people believe, being successful does not necessarily mean coming out of the other side having accomplished every goal, though this is important as well. If you are constantly hitting milestones, no matter how small they are, it is alright to consider yourself a success. This is because, rather than success being confined to an outcome...

Success is actually a habit, more than anything else

Success is the progressive realization of a worthy ideal. It is impossible to make progressive steps without having a set of habits in place to prop it up. It is habits which decide the quality of the person and by extension, the quality of the person's life. It could be any part of life; if you are consistent in reading books daily it is obvious that you would be more knowledgeable than most of the people in your group. If you make it a habit to exercise and maintain a healthy diet, your body generally would tone up and show the relevant results. So, a man, or woman, is nothing but his or her habits.

Forming new habits will require you to exercise self-discipline

Funnily enough... self-discipline is all about habits, and habit-forming. Self-discipline is that process of building specific habits over a period of time, which will assist you in obtaining a desirable outcome, a goal or an objective. In other words, we could say that self-discipline is all about taking small-sized, steady actions which will help to form habits, which subsequently help you reach your objectives and goals.

Self-discipline really is a process of steady, repetitive revision, regulation, correction and elimination of behavior, as opposed to simply hammering away at routines and actions, without having your mindset as your focal point of action:

When we talk about steady, repetitive revision, regulation, correction, and elimination of behavior, this is necessary to adapt to the changing conditions and circumstances in your environment. And you better believe it; your conditions will shift and change constantly, thereby requiring you to adapt to them and change your routines and patterns as well.

Habit-related questions that you should ask yourself so as to make your 'progressive realization of an ideal' possible:

46. What new habits should I follow to achieve this goal? List them

This is the first step, as far as habit-forming goes. *What new habits do you need to take up?* The 'what' is almost always linked to the 'why', especially where habit-forming is concerned. Once you identify the habit that you would like to take up, ask yourself why it is necessary for you to take it up. If you can answer this comprehensively, then the habit is indeed necessary to build. However, there is another dimension to habit-forming.

To effectively build new habits, it is necessary to destroy some old ones. If you want to develop the habit of promptness and respect for time, then you need to break the habits of procrastination and slothfulness.

You have to break these negative habits so that you stand a better chance of building new positive habits. If you want to build a habit of waking up at the crack of dawn and working through the morning, then you need to break the habit of sleeping late. If you want to build a habit of working in 25-minute periods without any distraction, you have to work on breaking your habit of checking your phone for social media updates every few minutes.

47. What would remind you to stick with the plan?

There are so many options here, that you are spoilt for choice. A reminder can be as simple as a timetable tacked at the corner of your desk; it could be as simple as your list of goals displayed somewhere that is easily viewable from your workstation.

Basically, it is necessary to have something motivational in place to remind you to stick to your plan and keep working even when you don't want to. *Have you seen boxers and martial arts fighters carrying photographs of family members who mean the world to them, and add to their motivation, to the ring?* This allows them to add to their psychological edge- even when they are in trouble; battered, hurt and exhausted, these 'photographs' help prop them up and keep them going even when they want to quit.

You have also seen CEOs and other leaders display photos of their family on their desk. Perhaps, you need a photo or two to keep you going. Really, a reminder could be anything. Figure out what works for you and then use it.

7. ACCOUNTABILITY QUESTIONS

The most effective people often have accountability partners to keep them on the 'straight and narrow.' An accountability partner does just what the name suggests; he/she helps in keeping you accountable.

Having an accountability partner will motivate you to move forward. He or she is basically a person who will push you when we feel down or low. This is the reason people have coaches who question them every week. Even the best coaches have their own personal coaches to progress.

Speaking of coaches, an accountability partner will be something of a coach to you. He/she will give you some encouragement when you need it. An accountability partner also reinforces the importance of every structure you have put in place to help you achieve your goal; he/she will make sure the timetable you draw up is followed to the letter; he/she will ensure that the workload that you have set apart for each day is met, Etc.

It is advisable to have an accountability buddy during the journey. There are some who succeed without one anyway, but an accountability partner makes it so much easier to be responsible and driven, and the added bonus of knowing that somebody else is invested in your dreams, to some level, also counts for something:

Here are the questions you need to ask yourself when you are screening potential accountability partners:

48. Whom will you associate with?

Basically, this points to multiple elements. *What character traits should your accountability partner exhibit?* You want a partner who shares some of your own character traits or projects a set of traits that you are working towards adopting.

Does the potential accountability partner have a track record of meeting his goals and smashing them? Look; an accountability partner who is a slacker in his or her own life will only transfer that slacker mentality onto your routine, which will only mean you end up worse off than you would have without an accountability partner.

Is the accountability partner a good person with a humane side to him/her? You may think this is a silly question to ask when screening for an accountability partner, but if you settle for a psychopath, no matter how effective and hardworking he/she is, how will they be able to invest their time and emotion in you and your goals when they do not have much of either left to spare for anyone else but themselves?

Examine the character and track record of your potential accountability partner so that once you make a choice, you will end up with a person who will offer the best support system.

49. Whose help is required for you?

This is yet another vital question you need to ask and answer. *Whose help do you really need?* This is what I mean by this question. Depending on who you are, and what your nature is, you may need a cheerleader in your corner, a vocal motivator, a quiet overseer who mostly stays behind the scenes while you do your thing, a person to hold your hand and help you overcome challenges and fear, a family member whom you share a deep emotional bond with, Etc. Only you know what works for you.

The first step to take, when seeking a definitive answer to this question, is to ask yourself what you need in terms of a support system. *What is your greatest distraction? What element has held you back the most from succeeding?* For instance, if your answer is procrastination, then you will need somebody who makes it very difficult to procrastinate such as a vocal motivator who checks in on you every so often to see how much progress you have made.

50. Whom will you call when you feel down or low?

You will certainly feel down at some point. You see, your brain is designed in such a way that it prioritizes short-term rewards over long-term ones. Thus, after repeatedly forcing yourself to work toward a long-term goal whose fruits you will not see immediately, you may notice that psyching yourself up for some intense work is often an uphill task, and you may feel some dread every time you prepare for a working session. In times such as these, you will need somebody you can call who will assure you that indeed, your goals and dreams are worth the effort you are putting in, regardless of the lack of immediate results.

There are times when external factors will get you feeling down. You could experience a crushing loss, or some things could demotivate you badly. But really, you have to shake all that off and get back to work if you are going to realize your dreams. It will help to have somebody to call or maybe just somebody to have a 5-minute coffee sit-down with. Just as a note, this person does not have to be the same person who you are accountable to, it can be somebody else.

51. Who is your coach?

Who is your coach? What would your coach do for you? Who is he/she? Does he/she have what it takes to cover all the facets of your pursuit? Does he/she have what it takes to get you to do what you need to do to achieve your goals? Can he or she hold you by the hand until you achieve your goals?

Answer the above questions and find a suitable person.

8. CELEBRATION QUESTIONS

At the end, it is about happiness. It is always about happiness. We set goals and targets just so we feel accomplished, successful and worthy. And there is no problem with any of this. This may include yourself and your surroundings as well. *How would you like to celebrate this victory? How would you like to reward yourself?* Setting celebration goals beforehand helps us to move forward with ease.

Here are some celebration questions to ask-

52. What were your biggest achievements this year?

Remember when we covered the goal-setting questions? One-month goals should add up to form 3-

month goals, which in turn add up to form 6-month goals; 6-month goals will add up to yearly goals, etc.

Have you managed to stay consistent with your mini-goals? If you have, then this particular question should be easy enough to answer. Acknowledge what your biggest achievements have been, the past year, and write them down. There is a sense of pride one feels when they are able to say with conviction that they completed something of some magnitude. Wear your accomplishments as a badge of honor- God knows you worked hard for them, as opposed to going the slacker route that most people opt for.

53. How would you celebrate once you achieve this goal?

You know what kind of person you are, and how you like your celebrations to look like. Perhaps, you are the introverted kind who likes to throw a party and have your friends and family share in your happiness. Perhaps, you are comfortable opening a bottle of cognac and enjoying it alone when you are in the mood to celebrate. One of the best ways to put a stamp to your celebratory endeavors is to reward yourself by spending a bit of money on you. Perhaps, you have desired a particular motorbike model, a branded purse, a set of new golf sticks, etc. Spoil yourself for a bit; you deserve it.

54. What are the milestone celebrations?

Milestones simply mean mini-goals. A monthly mini-goal represents a milestone, as does a 6-month mini-goal. It is important that you have some celebrations planned out for every milestone that you meet. *You may ask; why not put off celebrating until I have gone the whole hog?* But remember, this book defines success as the progressive realization of a worthy ideal. It does not say that success is the complete realization of a worthy ideal. Thus, every milestone you blast represents success. A mini-celebration should be in order.

55. Whom would you share this victory with once you have achieved?

It is important that you have someone dear to you join in your celebrations. This gives the whole event more magnitude. It adds substance and relevance to the event and confirms to you that indeed, your efforts were worthy, and your success, no matter how small, is nothing to scoff at.

There is also the small matter of feeling even more motivated to succeed once you involve another party, who proceeds to become invested in your success, at least to some degree. You can invite as many people as you want. You can simply call up your best friend, godfather, etc. You know what works for you.

CONCLUSION

Every question included in this book is geared toward helping you know *you* better, and be able to push yourself forward with more efficiency and grit. In case it wasn't obvious, this book pushes the very accurate message that you are indeed special and that you are unique and different from anybody else out there. You have unique tastes, mannerisms, goals and objectives; a unique background, a way of doing things and so much more.

If only you held yourself with the value that you deserve, and applied the requisite work, there is no way success would evade you. Take a hard look at every individual question, and try to answer as concisely as possible, and as this book has already recommended, make sure to write down each answer.

Soon enough, you will begin to see the fruits of your self-examination so that even your wildest dreams become normal things that you quickly get used to.

We have come to the end of the book. Thank you for reading and congratulations on reading until the end.

If you found the book valuable, can you recommend it to others? One way to do that is to post a review on Amazon. Visit Amazon orders page to leave your honest review of the book.

Check out my other books:

25 Small Habits,

50 things to realize

Comfortable slaves

Aligned work

Know Thyself

The Happy Couple

Thank you and good luck!